JB KING
Nelson, Maria.
Coretta Scott King / by
Maria Nelson.

Civil Rights Crusaders

CORETTA SCOTT KING

By Maria Nelson

Gareth Stevens
Publishing

Please visit our website, www.garethstevens.com. For a free color catalog of all our high-quality books, call toll free 1-800-542-2595 or fax 1-877-542-2596.

Library of Congress Cataloging-in-Publication Data

Nelson, Maria.
  Coretta Scott King / Maria Nelson.
     p. cm.— (Civil rights crusaders)
  Includes index.
  ISBN 978-1-4339-5680-5 (pbk.)
  ISBN 978-1-4339-5681-2 (6-pack)
  ISBN 978-1-4339-5678-2 (library binding)
  1. King, Coretta Scott, 1927-2006—Juvenile literature. 2. African American women civil rights workers—Biography—Juvenile literature. 3. Civil rights workers—United States—Biography—Juvenile literature. 4. African Americans—Biography—Juvenile literature. 5. King, Martin Luther, Jr., 1929-1968—Juvenile literature. 6. African Americans—Civil rights—History—20th century—Juvenile literature. 7. Civil rights movements—United States—History—20th century—Juvenile literature. I. Title.
  E185.97.K47N45 2011
  323.092—dc22
  [B]

                                    2010045998

First Edition

Published in 2012 by
Gareth Stevens Publishing
111 East 14th Street, Suite 349
New York, NY 10003

Copyright © 2012 Gareth Stevens Publishing

Designer: Katelyn E. Reynolds
Editor: Kristen Rajczak

Photo credits: Cover, pp. 3–24, back cover (background) Shutterstock.com; cover, p. 1 Richard Ellis/Getty Images; pp. 5, 7, 15 Hulton Archive/Getty Images; p. 9 AFP/AFP/Getty Images; p. 11 Michael Ochs Archives/Getty Images; p. 13 Robert Abbott Sengstacke/Getty Images; p. 17 Bob Parent/Hulton Archive/Getty Images; p. 19 Diana Walker/Time & Life Pictures/ Getty Images.

Printed in the United States of America

CPSIA compliance information: Batch #CS11GS: For further information contact Gareth Stevens, New York, New York at 1-800-542-2595.

CONTENTS

Words in the glossary appear in **bold** type the first time they are used in the text.

CIVIL RIGHTS LEADER

Coretta Scott King was a brave **civil rights** leader. She married Martin Luther King Jr. She helped him fight **segregation** in the South during the 1950s and 1960s. Later in her life, she gave speeches in favor of equal rights for women and peace all over the world. She stood up for those who were forgotten or mistreated. Coretta believed everyone should be listened to and respected, no matter what their race.

Coretta Scott King spoke at many events in her life, including the 1968 march on Washington organized by the Poor People's Campaign.

▽

5

EARLY LIFE

Coretta Scott was born in the small Alabama town of Heiberger on April 27, 1927. The South was still segregated then. Her family was poor. Coretta helped them by picking cotton and cleaning houses.

Coretta was smart. She graduated first in her class from Lincoln High School in 1945. Then, she studied music at Antioch College in Yellow Springs, Ohio, and the New England Conservatory of Music in Boston, Massachusetts.

LET FREEDOM RING

Coretta's high school had only black students. However, some of her teachers were white.

Coretta loved to sing and played the violin.

7

MARTIN LUTHER KING JR.

While in Boston, Coretta met Martin Luther King Jr. He was the son of a **minister** from Atlanta, Georgia. He was studying **theology** at Boston University. When Martin asked Coretta to marry him, she took a long time to decide. They married in the garden at the home of Coretta's parents on June 18, 1953. The wedding was a big event—350 guests came!

In 1954, the young couple moved to Montgomery, Alabama. There, Martin became a minister at the Dexter Avenue Baptist Church.

LET FREEDOM RING

Coretta's independence showed at her wedding. She wouldn't promise to obey her new husband in her wedding **vows.**

Coretta and Martin were married for almost 15 years.

9

THE KING FAMILY

Martin and Coretta had four children. Yolanda was born in 1955 and Martin III in 1957. The family moved to Atlanta in 1960. Dexter was born in 1961, then Bernice in 1963. Martin wanted Coretta to stay home and care for the children, but that didn't stop her. The couple traveled the world together. They saw poor people in Mexico and visited India to learn about Indian peacemaker Mahatma Gandhi. These trips had a great **impact** on Coretta.

LET FREEDOM RING

During her life, Coretta met with important people such as the famous South African leader Nelson Mandela.

The Kings' oldest child, Yolanda, was born in Alabama. She would grow up to be a civil rights speaker, too.

▽

JOINING THE MOVEMENT

Coretta joined in Martin's civil rights work early in their marriage. Like her husband, she believed in **equality** between blacks and whites. She took part in the bus **boycott** in Montgomery, Alabama. The law said blacks had to ride in the back of the bus. During the boycott, many blacks stopped riding buses until they could sit wherever they wanted. Coretta also arranged and took part in Freedom Concerts to raise money for her husband's group, the Southern Christian Leadership Conference.

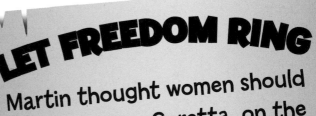

LET FREEDOM RING

Martin thought women should stay at home. Coretta, on the other hand, wanted to work for the civil rights movement alongside her husband.

The Kings, shown here holding hands at the front of the group, led a march in support of voter rights in early 1965.

▽

THE ASSASSINATION

Martin Luther King Jr. was **assassinated** on April 4, 1968. He left behind a continuing fight for equality. A few people seemed suitable for taking over Martin's leadership position. However, no one stepped forward. Coretta had four children to care for, but she didn't want her husband's work to end. Right after Martin's death, she took his place at a march in Memphis, Tennessee. She also spoke at the Lincoln Memorial for the Poor People's Campaign.

LET FREEDOM RING

The march in Memphis was to support black **sanitation** workers who were on strike. The strikers wanted better pay and safer working conditions.

Coretta and her children held Martin's funeral at Ebenezer Baptist Church in Atlanta, Georgia.

TAKING OVER

Coretta realized she was the best person to pass on Martin's message. She believed the country needed to change. She had also taken part in events supporting the Civil Rights Act of 1964. At first, she used parts of Martin's famous speeches about racial equality when she spoke. Then, she figured out her own message—she wanted everyone to be equal! Coretta spent the rest of her life working for civil rights for all, especially women.

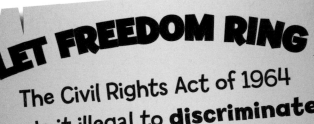

LET FREEDOM RING

The Civil Rights Act of 1964 made it illegal to **discriminate** against anyone based on race, beliefs, or whether they are a man or a woman.

Coretta marched with César Chávez in support of better conditions for farmworkers in the early 1970s.

▽

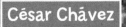

César Chávez

FARMWORKERS SAY
BOYCOTT LETTUCE
DON'T SHOP AT A&P

FARMWORKERS SAY
BOYCOTT LETTUCE
DON'T SHOP AT A&P

HONORING MARTIN

Coretta also spent a lot of time remembering her husband. In 1969, she published a book, *My Life with Martin Luther King, Jr.* Then, she founded the Martin Luther King Jr. Center for Nonviolent Social Change in Atlanta. The King Center is a **memorial** and a place to learn about Martin's message. Coretta started working on it soon after her husband's death.

In January 1986, Coretta accomplished another goal of hers—to make Martin's birthday a national holiday.

LET FREEDOM RING

The King Center has the largest library of papers from the civil rights movement.

President Ronald Reagan, center, invited the King family to witness the signing of the bill that made Martin Luther King Jr. Day a national holiday.

EQUALITY FOR ALL

Coretta formed many groups that fought for equality, including the Full Employment Action Council in 1974 and the Coalition of Conscience in 1983. Coretta met with peacemakers from all over the world. When she died in 2006, about 10,000 people attended her funeral.

Coretta was married to Martin Luther King Jr.—but that's not all she did in her life. She was a civil rights **crusader** in her own right.

LET FREEDOM RING

Four US presidents attended Coretta's funeral: Jimmy Carter, George H. W. Bush, Bill Clinton, and George W. Bush.

TIMELINE

1927	Coretta Scott is born on April 27.
1945	Coretta graduates from high school.
1953	Coretta marries Martin Luther King Jr. on June 18.
1964	The Civil Rights Act passes.
1968	Martin is assassinated on April 4.
1969	*My Life with Martin Luther King, Jr.* is published.
1981	The King Center opens.
1986	Martin Luther King Jr. Day becomes a national holiday.
2006	Coretta Scott King dies on January 30.

GLOSSARY

assassinate: to kill someone, especially a public figure

boycott: the act of refusing to have dealings with a person or business in order to force change

civil rights: the freedoms granted to us by law

crusader: a person who fights for a cause

discriminate: to treat people differently because of race or beliefs

equality: being treated the same and given the same freedoms

impact: strong effect

memorial: a place, display, or event that serves as a way to remember someone

minister: a person who leads a church service

sanitation: the collecting and getting rid of garbage

segregation: the forced separation of races or classes

theology: the study of God and faith

vows: promises

FOR MORE INFORMATION

Books

Farris, Christine King. *March On! The Day My Brother Martin Changed the World.* New York, NY: Scholastic Press, 2008.

Hardy, Sheila Jackson. *Extraordinary People of the Civil Rights Movement.* New York, NY: Children's Press, 2007.

Mis, Melody S. *Meet Coretta Scott King.* New York, NY: PowerKids Press, 2008.

Websites

Civil Rights Movement
www.neok12.com/Civil-Rights-Movement.htm
Watch videos about the history of the civil rights movement.

Stand Up for Your Rights
pbskids.org/wayback/civilrights/
Learn more about your civil rights and the people who fought for them.

Publisher's note to educators and parents: Our editors have carefully reviewed these websites to ensure that they are suitable for students. Many websites change frequently, however, and we cannot guarantee that a site's future contents will continue to meet our high standards of quality and educational value. Be advised that students should be closely supervised whenever they access the Internet.

INDEX